JUST JESUS AND ME

A Three-Year Journey

to Divine Healing and Salvation

DELPHINE KIRKLAND

Dedication

I dedicate this book to my immediate family—my father and mother, Anderson and Daphne Paige; my grandmother, Lillian Crim; and my brothers, Anderson Paige, Jr., and Andrew James Paige.

I was perfectly aware you didn't understand my unfaltering and unwavering decision at the time. Matter of fact, you didn't ask to be a part of my journey, but you got on board anyway. As my caregivers, your eyes beheld some horrifying, traumatic, and agonizing moments, but you never complained. You did what family members are supposed to do, and you gave me love and compassion. I will cherish your warm-heartedness for the rest of my life.

I love you,

Delphine

Table of Contents

Foreword

by Pangeline J. Edwards

I used to have faith, the kind of faith that changed the atmosphere each time I spoke. I had faith that moved mountains, giants, and other big obstacles that came my way. Then one day my father died, next my brother, then a dear friend taken in her youth, the big blow of my mother, and a year later my friend and mentor, a mighty woman of God, taken. And along with all this loss went my faith. Little by little, until one day I did not believe that God was as awesome as I thought He was.

The Almighty God, in my eyes, was no longer all mighty. Because if He was, He would not allow me to go through so much pain, hurt, suffering, and loneliness. Why would a loving God put me through all this heartache and brokenness so that I didn't even want to hear anything about Him, or have someone tell me how good He is, or be in the company of people who only had good things to say about this great big God. I didn't want to hear anything. I was in pain and I just wanted to be left alone.

Those who know me well will be in shock. Why? Because I eat, drink, sleep, breathe, and have my very being in Him. They know that God's word has kept me sane when the world wanted me to go crazy. Every time something catastrophic or challenging came my way, I was able to stand strong on the words I had read, scriptures I had memorized, and the testimonies of those whose faith in God helped them through their trying times.

So, when I hit rock bottom over and again, I was able to lift myself up. Until one day, after one too many challenges, too many setbacks, obstacles coming one after another, death upon death, pain upon hurt, upon depression, upon anxiety, upon grief, upon numbness. And for the second time in my life, I had a breakdown. Full-fledged, everything done, can't take another step, nervous breakdown.

Even though I knew the symptoms and read all the signs, there was nothing I could do. I could not stop it. I could not hold it back. I didn't have the energy. I had the knowledge to get through my mental and physical breakdown, but I was just too tired. Overwhelmed, I gave in.

Delphine did not give in.

I did not know Delphine's story when she asked me to write the foreword for her book. I did not know anything about her past. I did not know anything about her book. What I did know was that at the time of two of my greatest losses and decreasing faith, God put her in my life. One day I called Delphine, or perhaps she called me. I don't recall. I needed prayer and she was the one to pray for me.

Even though we were in two different states and the prayer was over the phone line, I knew it was a prayer warrior who was raising her voice for me, opening up the floodgates of heaven so that my mind, body, spirit, and soul could be healed by the greatest healer who had ever walked on this earth.

You know when you are in the presence of a prayer warrior. That person's prayers are different from regular prayers. When a prayer warrior steps into the room, the atmosphere changes. Their prayers are answered before they utter their first word. Why? Because they have spent countless hours with God to the point where, like Moses, the glory of God upon them is so bright, that you are afraid to look at their face. (Exodus 34:29-30).

Without the glory of God in your life, there is total chaos. You lack structure, purpose, and meaning. We need the glory so we can be connected to God. Delphine knows the importance of a close walk with God. I had forgotten and needed a wake-up call.

As I read through *Just Jesus and Me: A Three-Year Journey to Divine Healing and Salvation,* these words jumped out of the page at me: "Sometimes our trials bring out the best and worst of us, which we need to see." If you ever felt for one minute that you have lost your faith in God, this book will guide you back. If you believe you have no faith and desire to get some, then this book will teach you how to get, increase, and keep your faith. If you, like me, have succumbed to the cares of the world and have only mustard seed faith, then this book will bring you back to your first love and the walk with God you so badly desire again.

Just Jesus and Me is a book on prayer and faith, but more than that it is a book about courage. It takes courage to hold fast to your belief, especially when everyone around you is speaking words of doubt and instilling fear. It takes courage to push through even when your own body and mind are fighting you to stop and give in. It takes courage to persevere to the end.

If there is ever a time that you and I need to read this book, as well as get it into the hands of our friends and loved ones, it is now. Faith moves mountains and this world is facing a mountain of issues that need to be dealt with. Prayer changes things and it will take fervent prayer from the mouths of mighty prayer warriors to call upon the name of God so He will move His hand. Courage is taking action despite your fears, or how things look, and how they feel. When you finish reading this book, you will possess all three and so much more.

Pangeline J. Edwards

August 11, 2019

A Message from Delphine

We live each day, not knowing what life has in store for us. Whether we are saved by grace or a sinner in need of a Savior, life doesn't care. We are in this world but not of this world. Life can be evil, brutal, merciless, and unrelenting. As children of the Most High God, we anticipate our lives to be attacked and battered by Satan's devices. The problem is, we don't know when and sometimes we don't know why he is attacking us. Rest assured, Satan has a contract on us and his mission is to kill, steal and destroy. However, we have a Savior that can defeat any weapons formed against us, and His name is Jesus.

This book will help you find peace in God when your world is turned upside down, and how to fight the good fight of faith. It'll show you how to stand when no one is standing with you, how to hold on when the flesh wants to give up, how to recognize the deceptions and trickery of the enemy, the true meaning of a prayer warrior, and how to appreciate God's mercy and grace when you know you don't deserve it.

I pray you will feel God's presence and experience His undying love for you as you read each chapter.

My main purpose for writing this book was not to become a bestselling author and to make millions but to help and bless a soul in need of the Lord. If a soul can be saved or touched by this book, my writing will not have been in vain.

Be blessed,

Delphine

CHAPTER ONE

I'm Going to Hell!

Raised in a Christian home had its benefits. One particular benefit was weekly Bible study at home.

Did you have Bible study in your home? I did. Every Tuesday night, the Paige family had Bible study and prayer meeting in their home. Mom and I would sing songs, and Daddy would bring the Word. Yes, I had two Bible studies in a week. I pretended I played the piano on the windowsill, and when I played the prelude of the song, I instructed my family to sing. Afterward, we prayed, and Daddy taught us a Scripture from the Bible.

Some Tuesdays, Mom had to work the night shift and missed meetings. One particular night, Daddy taught the Scripture, "Thou Shall Not Steal." He defined different ways a man could steal, and the more he talked, the more afraid I became. I was nervous and restless. My brothers sat quietly and listened carefully to what Daddy had to say. My hands sweated and my heart beat rapidly. After the prayer meeting was over, we went to bed.

I was scared and frightened after Daddy told us about stealing. All I could hear was him saying that stealing was a sin and if you break God's commandments, we would go to hell. Why was I so nervous? You see, the night before, I went into the kitchen and stole a cookie from the cookie jar without asking my parents if I could have one. We were raised to ask for something before taking it. I knew Daddy didn't know because I heard him snoring down the hall. Mom was at work and my brothers were asleep, so how could anybody tell Daddy what I had done?

My little six-year-old mind wasn't aware that God sees and knows everything we say and do. I was told that God sits high and looks low, but I didn't think He saw me. The Bible speaks of a holy watcher in **Daniel 4:13.** I didn't know about this holy watcher and wondered if God was watching me. In my heart, I felt bad about what I had done. I saw me burning in hell, and I was too scared to close my eyes. I was horrified that I was going to die that night. I didn't want to go to hell.

Hours later, I heard my mother drive up the driveway and unlock the back door. She wandered around the kitchen for a few minutes and then went to my brothers' room. Later, she entered my room and turned on the light to see a six-year-old girl sitting in the middle of her bed, eyes fiery red and silently crying.

"Delphine!" she screamed. "What's wrong with you?"

I looked at her with tears rolling down my face and said, "I'm going to Hell!"

Immediately, she wrapped me in her arms and comforted me, asking me to explain. I confessed stealing the cookie from the cookie jar and how Daddy had said that if we stole, we would go to hell.

"Anderson! Anderson!" Mom angrily screamed for my daddy.

Dad quickly entered my room.

There I was, crying, trembling, and scared, feeling as if there was no hope.

Mom relayed my story and reminded him of an important piece of information he should have mentioned if we had sinned. She told him to explain the Scripture about confessing our sins.

The Bible tells us in **I John 1:9, "If we confess our sins, he is faithful and just to forgive us our sins, and to cleanse us from all unrighteousness."**

Dad sat next to me on the bed and said if I confessed my stealing, that God would forgive my sin. I immediately confessed, went to bed peacefully, and watched my mother looking at my father not so peacefully.

That was my first experience of conviction. That was the first time I found myself in the Word of God and felt convicted and sorry for my sin. What an experience. That's what we are supposed to do when we find ourselves living short of His Word.

John the Baptist told the people standing around Jordan, when they found themselves in the Word which he preached, what they could do about their wrongdoings. The sinners, publicans, and soldiers cried out to John and asked, **"What shall we do then?" (Luke 3:8-14).**

If Daddy had told me what I could have done whenever I sinned and how to get it right with God, I wouldn't have felt I was doomed. I learned a valuable lesson that night.

Have you ever felt that way? Have you ever felt your sins were too horrible or you were so ashamed of what you'd done that God would not forgive you? Please don't feel that way. The devil wants us to think that God is not a forgiving God and will hold a sin over our heads to the time of judgment. The reason he wants to deceive us is that he doesn't want us confessing and asking for forgiveness. He wants the sin to remain.

Confessing your sins to God and asking for forgiveness removes the sins from you.

If you need to confess your sins and ask God for forgiveness, do it now. Don't give Satan the pleasure of tormenting your mind, heart, and soul any longer. Jesus told the woman who was found in adultery to go and sin no more **(John 8:11)**.

God wants us to confess our sins and not die in them. **"I said therefore unto you, that ye shall die in your sins: for if ye believe not that I am he, ye shall die in your sins" (John 8:24)**. That's what He is telling us to do. Whatever sin you were committing, don't be found in that sin anymore.

CHAPTER TWO

Mommy, I Can't Breathe

Asthma was my enemy. I was born with asthma, and several times it nearly took my life. If you are fortunate to have a praying mother and father, count yourself blessed. Prayer is the foundation of the family.

Whenever I felt the shortness of breath and the tightness of my chest late at night, I cried out to my mother. "I can't breathe, Mommy." Mom would run down the hall, pick me up, and take me outside to inhale the night air. As she gently held me in her arms, I always heard her talking. She called the name Jesus; sometimes, Heavenly Father.

With tears rolling down my cheeks, I saw my father looking out the back door, watching Mom talking and singing to me. Dad had to get up early in the morning to walk to work, but he never left until I was all right. I love him for that.

When the asthma attacks were severe, Mom and Dad loaded me in the car to take me to the hospital. The next morning, I'd wake up in an oxygen tent.

Whenever I had an attack during the school season, my first- through third-grade teachers visited and tutored me so I wouldn't get behind in my classes. I miss those types of teachers.

I suffered from asthma for years until the age of nineteen when I had my last attack. I had friends who had asthma who are no longer with me. My elders told me I grew out of it. I felt they were right, so I accepted what they told me. Later, I found out who was behind my recovery.

I grew up hearing my parents singing and praying to God. I heard the names Jesus, Lord, God, Savior, and Heavenly Father coming from my parents' mouths, whether things were good or bad. Sometimes, Mom would be in the kitchen washing dishes and talking, and I would look to see who she was talking to, but no one was in the room but her. Matter of fact, my grandmother would do the same thing.

I was confused for quite some time. I would go back to my bedroom and wonder who Mom had been talking to. Was she losing her mind? I didn't know she was talking to Jesus, the one who died for me and later saved me.

I thought when you talked to Jesus, you had to be on your knees. Keeping a prayer in your heart was a way to pray to God. The true meaning of praying to God was something I found out years later. I'm so grateful I had parents who called on Jesus to heal me and help me.

Prayer wasn't an option in my childhood; it was a must. When kneeling by my bed as a child, I didn't fully understand why Mom sat on my bed each night to teach me the Lord's Prayer. Ending the day with a prayer on our lips was mandatory in our household, and I learned how important it was. Mom, Dad, and my grandmother taught me that God will hear our prayers anytime and anywhere, whether we are on our knees or not.

CHAPTER THREE

Bullying Taught Me How to
Pray and Forgive

In the book of Job, **"the Lord said unto Satan, Whence comest thou? Satan answered and told God he was going to and fro in the earth and from walking up and down in it. The Lord said unto Satan, have you considered my servant Job? Satan reminded God that a hedge was around Job, his house, all that he had"** (Job 1:6-12).

As children of God, we sometimes forget that Satan knows God shields and protects us, but when the hedge is moved, whether God moves it or we walk out of the boundaries, Satan can steal, kill, and destroy. Satan nearly tried to destroy Job's life and God gave him permission. Was God cruel? No. Sometimes our trials bring out the best and worst of us, which we need to see.

Many lives have been taken because of bullying. It saddens me to see someone bullying another person. I experienced bullying in my childhood. The first time was when my oldest brother, Anderson, was bullied. He is a little person. Back in the day, he was called a midget or a dwarf. I never knew he was different until I saw little people at the circus. I couldn't understand why people laughed at them because they looked like my brother. I never laughed at him.

My brother's bullying began when he started school. He came home crying and begging Mom not to make him go back. My brother Andrew and I witnessed this almost every day of the week. Andrew said watching his brother constantly crying was so heartbreaking. His elementary teachers did a good job protecting him; however, when he went to junior high and high school, the bullying worsened.

I loved my brother, and it hurt me to see him crying. He told us how they would repeatedly hit his head, mock him, and make up silly names to embarrass him. During my teenage years, I wanted to fight for him. I dared someone to laugh or make fun of him in my presence. If we were out for dinner, I confronted people who stared or insulted him.

I asked God to help my brother whenever he had to go anywhere. The more my brother returned home crying, the madder I became. I prayed more often. I wanted God to stop it, but it seemed as though it was taking too long for Him to stop those bullies. I was truly in need of patience.

As years passed, I noticed my brother wasn't crying as much. One day, we passed a group of teenagers who called him unfriendly names. I was about to rouse them up, but he stopped me. He said to forgive them. "They don't know what they are doing."

I looked at him in total disbelief because his face was peaceful. I knew he was quoting the scripture of Luke 23:34, where Jesus told his Father to forgive the people for wrongfully mistreating him. At the same time, I was dealing with bullies, too, but I was unable to say that. I couldn't understand the peace I saw on his face. Whenever I was with him, he wasn't as angry or as hurt. I didn't know he was showing me the power of overcoming the enemy and the power of forgiveness.

Not only was asthma my enemy, but I had another enemy called eczema. After researching the cause of eczema, I discovered that people with eczema often have allergies or asthma. I had allergic reactions to chocolate and tomatoes. I loved them both, but they didn't love me. My skin was dry and scaly, and the itch was intense. My body was covered with small bumps and leaked fluid when I scratched. The itchy bumps popped up on my skin, and the fluid-filled blisters oozed and crusted over. I cried constantly because of the burning and stinging pain.

Mom took me to countless doctors, who prescribed various types of medicated cream that soothed momentarily but never healed me. I was ashamed to go out in public, especially to school.

I'd heard the Scripture in **Romans 8:28: "And we know that all things work together for good to them that love God, to them who are the called according to his purpose."**

As a teenager suffering from so much pain, I couldn't see any good in that. I loved God and asked, "What good will this suffering do for me?"

My eczema introduced me to my first bully, Ronald. In elementary school, the teachers sat us alphabetically by our last names, so I ended up sitting next to him from first grade to the sixth grade. Because I was in and out of the hospital as a result of asthma attacks from the first and third grade, I wasn't in class much. The bullying started in the fourth grade.

I tried covering my blisters, but in the warm seasons, I couldn't hide my scaly skin. Ronald noticed the blisters around my neck and laughed. I ran home crying of embarrassment. As soon as Mom heard about it, she immediately told his mother, but it didn't do any good.

My grandmother Lillian was a prayer warrior and always prayed. We called our grandmother, "Big Momma." I told Big Momma how

Ronald laughed at my rash, which caused the other boys to tease me. Big Momma encouraged me to return to school and hold my head up high. I thought my grandmother had lost her mind. How can you hold your head up high when your heart is so heavy? It wasn't easy to do, but I knew Big Momma was praying for me.

My grandmother reminded me daily that she was praying for me, but the more she prayed, Ronald's bullying worsened. The teachers told him to stop, but he was mischievous and started bullying me off the school campus.

Although Big Momma was praying, I felt she needed help. Before and after school, I cried out to the Lord. My heart ached. I was broken. I didn't ask for eczema, but it chose me. So many times, I thought about my brother Anderson. He didn't ask to be born a little person, and other people didn't ask to be born with mental, emotional, and physical challenges or suffer years of bullying. God didn't make a mistake when He made us. Whether you were born with one leg or no legs, one arm or no arms, God loves you just the same.

When the disciples saw the blind man, they asked Jesus if the reason he was born blind was that his parents had sinned. Jesus said neither had the man nor his parents sinned, but it was for God's work to be made manifest in him. He told the disciples, **"I must work the works** of him that sent me" (John 9:1-4). God's work will be manifest in the lives of some of you who have been victims of bullying.

I didn't think bullying was fair. My heart was deeply broken. Little did I know the Word of God said, **"The Lord is nigh unto them that are of a broken heart, and saveth such as be of a contrite spirit"** (Psalm 34:17).

I hadn't known, but I still prayed. I couldn't stop praying because the pain was hard to bear. The Word of God tells us to pray without ceasing and the effectual prayer of a righteous man availeth much (James 5:16/I Thessalonians 5:17).

That experience taught me that no matter how broken you are, keep praying. Never cease from praying, and God will answer your prayer. I was angry and hurt when my brother was bullied, but I couldn't relate to the depth of his feelings until I was bullied. I learned to have compassion whenever someone is hurting, and I don't take their feelings lightly.

I wanted God to stop Ronald the first day, but he didn't. God knows how much we can bear, and He knows when and how to lift our burdens. Did Ronald stop bullying me? No. However, the prayers made me stronger, and Ronald's bullying words didn't affect me like they used to. I became dead to his harsh words. A dead man doesn't feel anymore, and God helped me to defeat the enemy.

I realize now that when you show the devil that he doesn't have power over you, he will leave you alone. The devil tried tempting Jesus and realized he had no power over him, and he left him alone **(Matthew 4:11).**

Jesus was tempted by the devil to turn stones into bread, worship him, and prove he was the son of God by throwing himself down from the top of the temple. Jesus refused. After Jesus rebuked Satan, the devil left him and the angels came and ministered unto him **(Matthew 4:1-11).**

God chose to answer my prayer according to His will and His timing. He wanted to give me power over my enemy. That was the best thing to do because I've met many Ronalds in my life since then, and that childhood experience was a blessing.

What did I learn from this? God can easily stop the hands of Satan, but God wants us to master Satan and his cunning schemes. I didn't know that was God's purpose for me then, but now I know. All things worked for the good in that situation.

Have you ever prayed for a long period for God to move on your behalf and it seemed to take too long? Patience goes with praying. The Bible tells us that God shall avenge his own elect, which cry day and night unto him, though he bear long with it. God will avenge them speedily, too **(Luke 18:7-8).**

Are you being mentally, physically or verbally abused? Are you being molested? Do you have a bully? Please don't take your life. You are the victim, but God can make you the victor and the conqueror. Tell someone; don't keep this a secret. Seek for help in more than one way just in case those you reached out to don't believe you. Someone will believe you. Ask God to help you and reveal your abuser or molester. Keep praying. God hears your prayers and sees your abuser, molester, and bullies. Watch how He will deliver you. Don't stop praying.

CHAPTER FOUR

His Plans Were Not My Plans

Approaching my last year in college, I had to make a big decision about whether to stay in school. I became sick, both mentally and physically. I was stressed out from singing engagements, choir tours, and class overload. I was fighting suicidal thoughts.

The suicidal thoughts scared me, and I needed help. This was my last year. I wanted to become an opera singer and travel around the world, but it looked like that was not going to happen. I was breaking out in small measles-like bumps, and suicidal thoughts were increasing.

I had never had a desire to take my life, and it was frightening. The doctor I was seeing recommended I see a psychiatrist. My grandmother always encouraged me that if I had a problem, talk to Jesus. I had to talk to God like Mom had when she was washing dishes or cleaning the house. I prayed mercifully to God and asked Him to remove those thoughts.

I wanted to finish college and make my dad proud. This daddy's girl didn't want to disappoint her father because he worked so hard to put me through school. That was important to me because the first time I saw Daddy disappointed was when Delores, my sister, died. After her death, I was smothered with extra love.

Don't get me wrong; my parents loved us all, but losing a daughter was hard, and they were overprotective of me.

I was blessed and highly favored to have a father who loved his family. He was a devoted husband and tried his best to take care of his family. He was not the type who expressed his love in words, but he was most certainly the kind who expressed it in works and deeds. Mom constantly reminded us that Daddy worked hard for us so we could have a roof over our heads, food on the table, and clothes on our backs. The more she reminded of us, the more I fell in love with my dad.

Every night, I heard him praying for us. He went to bed early because he had to walk about three miles to arrive at work on time. Many mornings, the smell of breakfast and him talking to Mom as she prepared his lunch woke me. I'd sit up in bed and wait to hear the back door shut. Daddy would walk by my window to meet the other fathers walking to work. I listened to his footsteps on the driveway pavement and sometimes watched him greet the other men as they headed up the pitch-dark road. I was saddened to see him walking in the mornings when it rained. Uppermost in my mind was how much my father loved me and did all this for me.

Around 3:00 in the afternoons, I'd rush to the front door because Daddy was coming home. I knew he must be tired, and I wanted to see him smile. After losing my sister, he didn't smile much, so I wanted to make him laugh again.

One afternoon, I patiently watched the road, waiting for the fathers. As soon as I saw one of the men, I was excited. And when I saw my Dad, I shouted, "There he is!"

I leaped off the steps and ran to meet him. I grabbed his hand, swinging it up and down and holding it tight. As soon as we entered the house, I led him to his favorite chair and took off his boots. His feet would be tired from walking, so I massaged them. I wanted him to know I appreciated how hard he worked for us.

All those years that Daddy worked, I never heard him complain. As a child, I was told if a man doesn't work, he doesn't eat. **"For ever when we were with you, this we commanded you, that if any would not work, neither should he eat"** (2 Thessalonians 3:10). Also, in 1 Timothy 5:8, it says, "But if any provide not for his own, and specially for those of his own house, he hath denied the faith and is worse than an infidel."

Oh my, how life has changed. An infidel, my dad was not. I admired what he did for us, and I didn't take his love for granted.

So, there I was, trying to decide whether I should stay in college or go home and rest for a semester. I was already seeing a doctor downtown, and the medication he prescribed wasn't helping. I had mixed feelings. What would people say or think about me? I was so close to finishing college, and what about my dreams of becoming an opera singer? I wanted to be another Marian Anderson or Leontyne Price.

I made my plans, not knowing His plans were not my plans and that God already had plans for me and I didn't know it. My classmates were graduating and had jobs of their dreams, and I didn't.

I asked my parents to come to see me on campus before making a decision. Mom and Dad visited and listened to my thoughts and wavering decisions. I'd always valued my father's opinion and asked him what I should do. For the first time, he wouldn't give me his opinion. *What?* Daddy was wise, and I knew he had the answer, but he left the decision in my hands.

I was uncomfortable because I had spent most of my years pleasing Daddy and other people, and many times I was miserable. Have you ever been that way? If a friend wanted something and I wanted it, too, I stepped back and let them have it. That's an unhealthy way to live.

Deep in my heart, I felt I needed to take a break, but I wanted to please my father. I thought he would be heartbroken or disappointed if I left school.

After deciding to leave college and take a break, my parents were pleased. Daddy wasn't disappointed. This taught me two lessons. One, don't live your life pleasing others and be unhappy; and second, don't allow Satan to trick you into thinking that a person is thinking one way when they're not thinking that way at all. Daddy wanted me to do what was best for me, and he respected my decision and opinion.

Returning home for a few months, my health issues haunted me in my dreams. What would people say and think? I slowly fell into a minor state of depression. I felt like a failure. Had I made the right decision? Perhaps I should have waited. These thoughts tormented me. I needed an answer and confirmation from God.

My brother, Andrew, was seeing a dermatologist and suggested I get an appointment to see this doctor for the small bumps that were increasingly spreading on my arms. I did so, and while sitting in the waiting room, I kept asking God if I had left college too soon.

When the doctor examined my arms, he asked what I'd been doing. His question confused me, and I asked what he meant. He wanted to know if I lived under a lot of stress. I shared with him my college days, and he said it was best to leave whatever was causing the breakouts.

An instant peace hit my heart because I knew that was my answer and my confirmation that I'd made the right choice. If you are ever in doubt about a decision you've made, always ask God to confirm it.

CHAPTER FIVE

Share Your Testimony

"So then faith cometh by hearing, and hearing by the word of God" (Romans 10:17).

I heard a dynamic testimony of faith one night, which changed my life. One evening after choir rehearsal, our musician Allen, a native of New York, came by the house for a visit. He noticed the tiny bumps on my arms and inquired about them. I told him I was trusting God to heal me.

He smiled and said I reminded him of a lady he knew in New York. He shared the story of this woman, who had cancer. She was tired of the weakness from chemo and radiation treatments, so she discontinued the treatments and trusted God to heal her. The lady stood in faith and on the Word of God, and God healed her body.

I was amazed. Allen had no idea that testimony planted a seed of faith in my heart and mind.

If you have a burning testimony, please share it. You have no idea who needs to hear it. I am so grateful that God allowed him to share that testimony because it changed my life. After that dynamic testimony and reading about miracles in the Bible, I wanted God to perform one for me. I couldn't believe how someone with a life-threatening illness stops medical treatments and trusts God to heal them. I had never heard of that.

I've read testimonies in the Bible, and the people were fascinated how Jesus healed and saved them, such as the woman who met Jesus at the well, spreading her experience with Jesus **(John 4).** She wanted the people of Samaria to come and see the man who revealed everything that she had done. She was so credible that many of the Samaritans went to seek Christ and were convinced she was telling them the truth. I wanted to seek Christ and see for myself if this could be possible for me.

What did I notice about myself after hearing this testimony? I learned of a woman who had faith in God and believed and trusted Him to heal her cancer. I was twenty-two years old and had attended church all my life. I went to vacation Bible school, Sunday school, and Bible study yearly, so why couldn't I believe that He couldn't heal me?

The Bible is real and people who received their healing were real, but they had something I didn't have and that was FAITH. My revelation was that no matter how much I attended church and other church events, if you don't believe God's Word or trust in Him, it doesn't matter. Just because you faithfully attend church doesn't mean you are a believer of the Word of God or have faith in God. No matter how you read the Word, you must believe and live the Word.

What is faith? The Bible says that faith is the substance of things hoped for and the evidence of things not seen. Faith is not only believing but knowing that God will and can do the things you request. The Bible tells us that Abraham staggered not at the promises of God and was strong in faith and giving glory to God. His faith never wavered. He praised and thanked God for his son without any evidence that God would give him a son. Why? Because the Bible tells us in **Romans 4:20-21** that Abraham was fully persuaded that what God had promised, He would be able to perform.

Abraham believed and knew God was not a liar. God promised Abraham a son and he believed Him; however, Sarah, his wife, had doubts. God told Abraham that when he returned unto him, Sarah would have a son. Sarah heard what was spoken and laughed within. Sarah was looking at the impossibilities instead of the possibilities. She and Abraham were **"old, and well stricken in age" (Genesis 24:1).**

Our age doesn't stop God from performing His Word. When Sarah laughed within, the laughter was silent because she laughed inside. God hears and sees our hearts and thoughts. One thing for sure, God knows us better than we know ourselves. After all, He made us. God is wise, and He knows our thoughts, feelings, ways, and the intent of our hearts. Our Heavenly Father searches our hearts and minds, and He knows whose hearts are toward or against Him.

"O Lord, thou hast searched me, and know me. Thou knowest my downsitting and mine uprising, thou understanding my thought afar off. Thou compassest my path and my lying down, and art acquainted with all my ways. For there is not a word in my tongue, but, lo, O Lord, thou knowest it altogether" (Psalm 139:1-4).

When Jesus told the man sick of the palsy that his sins were forgiven, certain scribes reasoned in their hearts. Jesus immediately perceived in His spirit that they were reasoning within themselves. Jesus asked why they were reasoning about what he had said in their hearts **(Mark 2: 5-11).** He knows when we believe and doubt.

Sarah didn't believe what the Lord had spoken, and the Lord questioned her gesture. She denied laughing because she was afraid. God asked a question: **"Is anything too hard for the Lord?" (Genesis 18:10-15).**

God promised Abraham a son and Sarah overheard it, but that was Abraham's promise, and sometimes you have to believe God's promises for you personally when others doubt you. Just as Abraham, you can be the only one in your household who believes in God while others have their doubts. You must let nobody and nothing shake your faith in God. This is something I had to learn to do, and I am still practicing it today.

CHAPTER SIX

I Had an Idea, or Was It God's Will?

Two months passed, and the tiny bumps on my skin were increasing and becoming very irritating. The medications were not working, and I was frustrated.

I prayed and asked God to heal me. I read my Bible more than ever. I learned that prayer and reading the Word of God is powerful. How? Reading the Word of God teaches you more about God. Why pray to someone you don't know?

I noticed in my reading that some of the people didn't know who Jesus was. Some heard about him by the hearing of the ear. That's how I learned about him. My parents told me about Jesus at an early age. I have never met Him personally. I was told that Jesus did perform those miracles.

Because I was praying about my skin disease, I read all the miracles about healing. The more I read, the more I believed it. I prayed and read, prayed and read, and I could visualize how those people looked and how happy they were after receiving their healing. If Jesus could do these miracles for them, could He do them for me?

As I read about the woman with the blood issue, the ten lepers, and how Job went through his trials back to back and kept the right spirit, I asked God to heal me. While reading about the people in the Bible who were miraculously healed, questions plagued my mind. What kind of people were they to receive these types of miracles? What kind of mindset did they have? How could Job praise God after losing his family, wealth, and suffering in his body? Ten lepers asked for healing, and Jesus told them to show themselves to the priest. **(Luke 17:11-19).**

What? Why? You ask Jesus to heal your sick servant and ask Him to speak healing over him and leave and go home. When the centurion returned home, his servant was healed? **(Matthew 8:5-13).**

Wait a minute!

I didn't know the answer to those questions then, but I do now. The answer is trust, faith, belief, and obedience. The ten lepers asked Jesus to heal them. They didn't question His answer, but they chose to obey because they trusted Him. Because of their obedience, they received their healing. Why would He tell them to go show themselves to the priest? An individual with leprosy was considered an outcast and labeled as unclean. He or she could not stay in their city of residence; the priest ordered the person to leave. By returning, the priest would witness the power of healing. The testimonies of God's healing were sure to spread abroad when the priest and the people in the city who knew of the lepers beheld their clear skin.

The centurion's faith was so powerful that he knew Jesus had the power to heal his servant. Jesus had the reputation of healing the sick and raising the dead. There was no doubt in his mind that Jesus had authority over life and death.

Jesus spoke, "Come forth," and Lazarus came out of the tomb. Before he told Jairus' daughter, "Talitha cumi," which is interpreted, "Damsel, I say unto thee, arise." He first moved the doubters out. Doubt ties God's hands and faith frees God's hands. After watching the mourners in the house weeping and wailing, He said, **"'Why make ye this ado, and weep? The damsel is not dead, but sleepeth.' And they laughed him to scorn. But when He had put them all out, he took the father and mother, Peter, James, and John with him and entered in where the damsel was lying" (Mark 5:35-43).**

What was Jesus doing? He was kicking out the doubters and bringing in those who had faith and believed Him. Jesus wanted to perform mighty miracles in his hometown, but he did not because of their unbelief (**Matthew 13:54-58**). Doubt hinders and interrupts God for performing healings and mighty miracles.

Are you hindering God? Do you have trouble believing God? Is there anything too hard for God? God can do anything according to His will. There is nothing too hard for God. Whenever doubters are amongst you, clean house. Kick out your doubters!

I had an idea to ask God for a task that He had done for those people He'd healed in the Bible. Was it an idea, or was it God's will? I don't know, but I hoped to find out.

Sometimes we think we have an idea or a plan, but all along, it was God's will. I thought about it seriously and prayed mightily about it. See, I read about His miracles, but I had personally never heard of anyone for whom God had done those things. I wanted to see for myself.

Allen's testimony inspired me to pursue an idea into reality. That's why I wrote this book: to share my testimony. Someone's testimony changed my life.

CHAPTER SEVEN

December 16, 1979

After Allen left that night, I couldn't stop thinking about the testimony from the cancer-stricken lady who had been healed. I went into my bedroom and gathered the medications from my dresser. I sat on the bed looking at all the medications I was taking and realized they weren't helping. I couldn't get that woman's astounding faith in God out of my mind.

For several minutes, I sat pondering. I decided I was going to make a vow. I had to sit a while before I made the vow because **Ecclesiastes 5:4-5** says, **"When thou vowest a vow unto God, defer not to pay it; for he hath no pleasure in fools: pay that which thou hast vowed. Better is it that thou shouldest not vow, and not pay it."**

I had to ensure I would be committed to this vow. Once I committed myself, I had to go through with it because I wanted to be healed and not let God down. Most of all, I didn't want to let myself down. I had to believe God with all my heart, mind, and soul and let nothing deter me. What I was about to embark on was serious, and it could make me or break me, so I had to think this through, carefully and spiritually.

It was late and everybody was asleep except me. I wasn't afraid of what I was about to do. I had to do this. Gathering my meds, I quietly entered the hallway. I didn't want to wake anyone because I wanted to concentrate on what I was about to tell God. I needed no distractions.

My brothers' room was next to the bathroom, and I hoped I wouldn't wake them. I also hoped no one would have to go to the bathroom while I was in there.

It seemed God was waiting for me. No one disturbed me. I flipped on the light switch and entered the bathroom. I opened up the pill bottles and dumped the contents down the commode. I unscrewed the cream medications and squeezed them out of the tubes and into the toilet.

After I flushed, I stepped back, stood in front of the mirror over the washbasin, and talked to God.

"I heard about You, but I really don't know You. I read that You can heal the sick and raise the dead, but I don't know You like that. I heard that You can open blind eyes, heal leprosy, and heal all kinds of diseases. If You are the same God of Moses who opened the Red Sea, prove yourself to me. The Bible says you are the same yesterday, and today, and forever (**Hebrews 13:8**).

"If you are the same God who raised Lazarus from the dead and opened the eyes of blind Bartimaeus, prove Yourself to me. Starting this day, December 16, 1979, I will not go to the doctor or accept any other medical treatments. I will trust You and wait on You to heal me."

After I finished talking to God, I left the bathroom and went to bed, excited to see what God would do.

I thought it would be appropriate to tell my parents and the rest of the household about my vow. I wanted them to see the mighty work of God and be a witness to what He was about to do for me.

One of my parent's responses was, "Yes, God can heal you." They were in prayer with me for my healing. I was so glad.

My two brothers didn't think much of it at the beginning because they knew I was always adventuring and trying out different things, but they were fine with it.

Okay! The household is with me, I thought.

A few months passed, and I noticed my skin was forming a fish-scale-like image. It was semi-hard and crusty.

I wasn't shaken. I kept saying to myself and my family, "God is going to heal me." But as I beheld my family members' faces, I saw signs of disbelief, but I couldn't allow their facial impressions to deter me. Just because I had been waiting a few months didn't mean God wouldn't heal me. I was still excited and told them and others that God was going to heal me.

CHAPTER EIGHT

No One Believes Me

Our family always attended Sunday school. One particular Sunday, the lesson was about healing. I was happy to express how God could heal because His Word tells us how he healed so many people in the Bible.

In class, I was more talkative than ever. When you truly believe something in your heart, you don't mind expressing it. You can't keep it to yourself. You want the world to know about it. I was like the woman at the well who had met Jesus, and when He told her everything about herself and blessed her, she wanted everyone to know.

I wanted everyone to know how God was going to heal me without any evidence. That's what faith is. "**Faith is the substance of things hoped for and the evidence of things not seen**" (Hebrews 11:1).

The superintendent rang the bell twice to notify the individual classes of our class time. The first bell alerted us that classes had ten minutes to wrap up, and the next bell was to adjourn in the sanctuary. I couldn't wait because after the superintendent reviewed the lesson, he asked if anybody had questions or comments. I had no questions, but I was full of comments.

After hearing the second ring, I leaped from my seat and raced to the sanctuary. I was so impatient that I prayed God would make the superintendent sit down so I could talk. Finally, he concluded his summary and asked if anyone had questions or comments. I quickly raised my hand and said, "Yes!"

As I ran to the podium, I was full of joy and couldn't wait to tell everyone the good news. I briefly shared with the congregation how I had stood and trusted God to heal my body. Many responded with an "amen." I was so happy.

But the happiness disappeared when I mentioned I wouldn't be receiving medical treatment and would wait on God for divine healing. It was as if I had shocked them. I was shocked at their response, as well. I only heard two faded sounds of "amen."

After I finished my message, I returned to my seat, feeling uncomfortable. I was talking to God in my heart and told God, *They don't believe me.* I was puzzled and couldn't understand.

Five months had passed and there were no changes, but I didn't mind because I kept trusting and believing. However, my parents minded.

When my skin disease spread between my fingers and formed small sores, my parents wanted to know if I needed to reconsider my decision.

I had no desire to change my mind. I was willing to wait and see what God would do. I had no doubt He could do it. I did not waver.

While the questions came, I realized they didn't believe as I believed. I had thought they were on board with me, but I soon found out they hadn't understood when I first explained my decision.

Mom was furious because she saw her daughter's body slowly covering with sores. She wanted me to go to the doctor. I was in my early twenties and of age to make my own decisions. My father told my mother to pull back and allow me to pursue my decision.

After church service one Sunday, I noticed my grandmother talking to the pastor of the church. Now and then, they glanced at me. Big Momma was up to something.

Later that day, our pastor arrived at our home. He was a good man, husband, and father. He expressed his concerns about my decision and recommended I go to the doctor. I explained that I had to know for myself that God could heal me. As he gave his point of view, my heart was hurting. *Of all the people, I thought my pastor would understand me.*

Maybe I was wrong, but aren't you supposed to believe in what you preach? I was utterly confused but not deterred from my healing journey.

Later that night before retiring to bed, I talked to the Lord about several things that troubled my heart. "They don't believe me, God." I was disappointed my family and friends didn't believe me, but I wasn't afraid. I was more determined than ever to show them what God could do.

Sometimes our disappointments are our blessings. I found out my disappointments became my strength. I told God, "I still trust you. I still believe in you, and I will wait on you."

The vow I made in the bathroom was between me and God. I didn't include anyone else. I had a vow to fulfill, not Mom, Dad, my brothers, or anyone else. Realizing that this was my personal walk allowed me not to get angry or bitter because others had doubts. I prayed harder because I realized I was not going to receive support on this journey, and I asked God to equip me for the task.

CHAPTER NINE

Just Jesus and Me

I was approaching the one year mark on my journey and repeatedly told myself and others that God was going to heal me. I saw doubtful hearts and read doubtful minds, but something inside me didn't care.

One night, I experienced pain between my lower right thighs. The next few days, a small bump grew. I could barely touch it and later realized it was a small boil.

Boils are extremely painful, and sometimes they grow larger until they are drained, so I immediately tried to administer first aid. I applied a warm compress to the area for fifteen to twenty minutes. While I nursed that one, another one formed under my armpits. I used Epsom salts to help the pus dry, but these boils were stubborn and pained constantly.

Sores began to break out inside and outside of both my arms. I wore long sleeves so my family wouldn't notice. I didn't want to hear them pleading with me to get medical treatment.

It was hard to walk with boils between my legs. Mom noticed my walk was different, so I had to tell her, but I assured her I had the situation under control.

I found myself living in my bedroom because walking around the house was painful. Thankfully, my dad purchased a television for my room for entertainment. My brother Andrew bought me magazines and books to read, and he humored me with jokes, knowing laughter was the best medicine. Although they didn't understand, they tried to make me comfortable and help. Isn't that what family is supposed to do?

While my mother worked in the mornings, my retired father prepared my meals, and my elder brother, Anderson, Jr., blessed me with a big smile every day when he brought meals to my bedside.

I thank God for my family. We worked together, and though they didn't quite understand my choice to wait on God, their love for their daughter and little sister was priceless. They went out of their way to make me comfortable. I knew they loved me, but on this journey, they showed me what it is to be there for family members, whether or not you agree or disagree with them.

Whenever I was able to attend church, I would, but sometimes the boils made it too painful to sit on the pews. Thank God for my godmother Ms. Omah Lee Jones, who was a seamstress. She made me skirts with flare tails, which enabled me to sit with my legs slightly open so the boils wouldn't touch.

The Lord put my godmothers in my life for a reason. Yes, I had three godmothers. God blessed me in such a way that I cannot explain. Ms. Omah Lee was a blessing, an amazing woman of wisdom, an excellent cook and baker, and the best friend anyone could have. Later, I will tell you more about this remarkable woman.

Disgusted! Disgusted! Disgusted! Why don't they believe me? The Bible is real! Lord, I know You and Jesus performed those miracles! I know God is healing me!

I quickly noticed my words. The first year, I told people, "God IS GOING TO HEAL ME." Going into the second year, I said, "God IS HEALING ME." There was no proof of my healing, but I believed God was doing something inside me without any evidence, and my mind and heart were changing into a level of faith that I did not know. I questioned the Lord, "Where is their faith? Don't they know you can do this?"

I grew up hearing people say that God could do anything, so why do these people doubt what I'm doing? I sought medical treatment, but there was no improvement, and since I'd decided to stand on His Word in faith, it seemed as though I was doing something wrong. I wished I could talk to Abraham or Job to find out what they did when those around them doubted. I had so many questions floating in my head.

One night, I talked to God and told Him that it was all right if nobody believed, for I did. This was not what I had expected. I thought everyone—my family and especially church members—would encourage me to trust God and be proud that I trusted and depended on Him. Instead, I was labeled as crazy by some, and boy did that hurt.

I even questioned God. One night, I asked Him, "Do you think I'm crazy to believe that You can do the same things for me that You've done for those in the Bible?"

I believe God created the heaven and the earth, made manna fall from heaven, and nothing was too hard for the Lord **(Exodus 16:3-4)**. I believe that Jesus raised Lazarus and the little boy lying lifeless in the coffin from the dead **(Luke 7:11-17)**. Jesus, indeed, opened the blind men's eyes, healed the ten lepers, and healed the sores and boils of Job.

I reflected on the Scripture in **II Timothy 1:12,** which says, **"For the which cause I also suffer these things: nevertheless I am not ashamed: for I know whom I have believed, and am persuaded that** he is able to keep that which I have committed unto him against that day."

This scripture was working for me at that moment. I was not ashamed to stand on faith and wait on God, regardless of what people thought about me. I believed. I really believed. God had persuaded me that he was able to keep His promises and perform what I had asked him. I was convinced that God would and could heal me.

The blind men asked Jesus to heal them. He asked if they believed that He could open their blind eyes. They responded, "Yes." Jesus told them, **"According to your faith be it unto you" (Matthew 9:29).**

It was all about our faith. The men's faith was strong. They heard that Jesus was healing the sick and raising the dead, and those men believed. It was about my faith. I heard and read the same thing. Jesus was a healer, and that's why I decided to trust God for my healing.

I had to walk and fight alone, so I told the Lord, "It's just You and me." I had finally realized it was going to be just Jesus and me on this journey. I wasn't angry at anyone, and I was no longer disappointed. Jesus and I were about to have a first anniversary on my journey, and He was still keeping me. I realized my journey was meant for me and that was fine.

I decided not to try to convince anyone anymore. If they believed me or didn't, it was okay. I didn't have an attitude and didn't think I needed to prove anything. I grew up in a house full of music and enjoyed Andrae Crouch's song, "I Got Confidence God's Going to See Me Through."

Andrae Crouch's music was a blessing to me during my trying times, especially the *Classic Gold: Live in London with The Disciples*. God spoke to me through his music. The song "Through It All" ministered to my soul numerous times.

I listened to religious programs on the Christian radio broadcast when I wasn't able to attend church. During the late nights of discomfort, the music of Sandi Patti, Russ Taff, The Imperials, Timothy Wright, Larnell Harris, The Hawkins family, The Gaithers, and Mahalia Jackson ministered to me and calmed my heart.

I concluded that my journey would only be with the help of the Lord. I sat up in bed one night and told Jesus, "It's just us. Just Jesus and me."

CHAPTER TEN

The Bible Was My Weapon

"For the word of God is quick, and powerful, and sharper than any two-edged sword, piercing even to the dividing asunder of soul and spirit, and of the joints and marrow, and is a discerner of the thoughts and intents of the heart" (Hebrews 4:12).

Day by day, there were changes to my body. My skin was getting slightly tight and turning darker. More sores popped up, and there were times I could hardly bend my knees.

My godmother Ms. Omah Lee told me to rebuke the devil when I was in pain or saw a new sore. "Tell the devil he is a liar."

I thought she had lost her mind.

I questioned her way of teaching. She shared how Jesus had rebuked the devil in Luke 4:10. I began to read the Bible religiously because I needed to know what Jesus said to the devil and apply that to my problems. That was my first lesson on how to rebuke the devil.

I noticed how Jesus talked to the devil, and it was with the Word of God. When the devil told Jesus to do something or offered him something, Jesus refused and said, "It is written."

All right, Lord! Okay, Jesus, now I understand. The devil doesn't tell you what to do, and you tell him what the Word of God tells you to do. I get it now. The devil doesn't dictate to you; you dictate to the devil. Get behind me, Satan!

God's Word was my weapon. Okay, Ms. Omah Lee, now I understand.

As children, we had to recite the Twenty-Third Psalm, and that was the first time I heard about anointing with oil. "**Thou anoinest my head with oil, my cup runneth over" (Psalm 23:5).**

I searched and studied the Scriptures. I read about the oil in the Bible. **Exodus 30:22-25: "Moreover, the Lord spake unto Moses, saying, take thou also unto thee principal spices, of pure myrrh five hundred shekels, and of sweet cinnamon half so much, even two hundred and fifty shekels, and of sweet calamus two hundred and fifty shekels, and of cassia five hundred shekels. And of cassia five hundred shekels, after the shekel of the sanctuary, and of oil olive an hin: and thou shalt make it an oil of holy ointment compound after the art of the apothecary: it shall be an holy anointing oil."**

54

I continued to do more research on oil. **James 5:14-15** states: **"Is any sick among you? Let him call for the elders of the church; and let them pray over him, anointing him with oil in the name of the Lord: And the prayer of faith shall save the sick, and the Lord shall raise him up; and if he have committed sins, they shall be forgiven him."**

"When I read the disciples went out two by two and cast out many devils, and anointed with oil many that were sick, and healed them" (Mark 6:7-13).

The church where I grew up did not anoint people with oil. I never witnessed any of my pastors praying and anointing with oil. I decided I'd purchase some oil to anoint myself. Mind you, this was all new to me. I didn't know what type of oil to buy because I had never read about a specific kind in the Bible. I knew oil was used for baking and cooking, but what kind for the skin? Should I purchase baby oil or mineral oil? I asked my godmother, and she suggested olive oil.

I had no idea God was using my godmother, who as a child attended a Holiness church, to lead and guide me on my journey. Mom purchased some olive oil, and I anointed myself every day. I didn't know how to anoint myself, so I used it as a lotion and rubbed my entire body with it.

This was a learning process because I was not taught in my church at the time to use oil and anoint myself. I had never seen anyone anointed with oil and prayed over, and I had no clue whether I was doing it correctly. I must admit this was strange and peculiar, but I tried to do what Jesus and the disciples did. Whenever the sores increased, I anointed myself and rebuked the devil.

God was in control of my journey. He put people in my life for reasons and seasons to help me along the way. One more blessing that Allen shared was introducing me to an evangelist named Shirley Brown. I have never heard a woman who could pray the fire of God down as she did. She received calls from me around the clock if I needed encouragement or prayer. Although I didn't want to disturb her late at nights or in the wee hours of the mornings, she was always ready to talk and pray with me as my body ached. She taught me about anointing myself with oil to a deeper depth. She never visited me but was dedicated to having Bible study with me on the phone and preached the Word of Faith to me. I was amazed she never complained when I constantly called her and woke her. She encouraged me to call because she said that was what she was there for.

CHAPTER ELEVEN

Pity Party or Faith Party. You Decide

It was getting harder to bend my arms. The sores in the pit of my arms wouldn't allow me to bend them well. Self-pity entered into my heart after hearing about my former schoolmates graduating from college. I should have been there, too, but instead, I was in bed, covered with sores.

What happened to the joy I had a year and a half ago? Instead of rejoicing, I was complaining. If you're planning on having a pity party, don't expect for God to show up.

One night, I sat in bed and had a pity party. "Seems as though everybody's achieving their dreams and goals except me," I said.

My student loan needed to be paid, and bills flooded in weekly. Knowing I was unable to work, the pity set in deeper.

I had a good cry. I couldn't ask God, "Why me?" I remembered what I had told God in the bathroom that night when I made that vow. God didn't make me do it or ask me; I did it on my own.

Immediately, I questioned myself. "Where is your joy, Delphine? A year and a half ago, you were so excited and told everyone that God was a healer and was going to heal you, so what's the problem now?"

My mind went back to a Scripture I had read in **Romans 4:20-21**, which explained how Abraham walked in faith for his unborn son. The Scripture says that Abraham was strong in faith, giving glory to God. I looked at my behavior and realized I was not strong that day; neither was I giving God the glory but giving the flesh the glory in self-pity.

Self-pity and feeling sorry for yourself does not move God, but praising and thanking God without murmuring, grumbling, and complaining moves God. Abraham did not have a pity party; he was too busy giving glory to God and was fully persuaded that the son God promised him would be given to him.

After realizing I was in the flesh and knowing the Scripture said that they who are in the flesh CANNOT please God, I felt embarrassed and cheap. Abraham was an old man, nearly a hundred years old, who praised and thanked God for a baby he had not seen, yet he believed God could do it. I was in my twenties and had proof from the Bible that God could do these things and I was complaining. Cheap! Cheap! Cheap!

I concluded that this pity party was coming to an end. I closed down the party and repented. I asked God to forgive me for wallowing in self-pity. I decided I would have a faith party and played uplifting gospel music and sang praises to God. The next thing I knew, I felt better and better about my situation.

I searched the Scriptures about faith and people who walked in faith and believed God. I was coming out of that old fleshly and carnal mind. The carnal mind was enmity against God. According to the Merriam-Webster dictionary, "enmity" means "deep-seated dislike or ill will."

If I'm carnal-minded, I have animosity and hatred against God and His Word. The fleshly mind hates and fights against the spiritual mind. You might have a mind to read God's Word, fast, or have a prayer group, and that fleshly mind will tell you all the reasons why you shouldn't read, fast, or set up a prayer group. But you know what? If you don't recognize what is going on, you will not see the tricks and traps of Satan. Watch and pray.

I had to be very careful to be alert and sober-minded because Satan slipped in and entertained me with those thoughts, and I went into that pity party without noticing.

Although Satan will come and tempt us, we must be spiritually alert as to what he does. Eve was not spiritually alert, and she believed every word the serpent planted in her mind. James 4:7 tells us to resist the devil, and he will flee. Eve didn't resist or rebuke, and the devil stayed in her presence telling lies. She believed him and missed out a great blessing from God. That taught me a valuable lesson about walking in the flesh and not in the spirit.

Oh, by the way, about the student loan. God prompted me to write to the president of the company and tell him the truth about why I was unable to make payments. I shared how I went to God that night in the bathroom and what I was doing at that time. I shared everything, not knowing what he would think. A few weeks later, I received a letter from the student loan company. I had expected a typed letter, but I pulled out a hand-written letter from the president of the company.

In the letter, the president told me that he admired my walk of faith. He was moved by my testimony and told me not to worry about the loan. He encouraged me to keep believing God and that he would remember me in his prayers.

My mouth flew open so wide that I screamed. When Mom raced into the room, I showed her the letter. "Look at God!"

After that, I never had another pity party. I no longer have that letter, but I wish I could tell the president that I'm healed.

CHAPTER TWELVE

I Don't Have Anything Against Doctors

At about the end of the second year, my legs were swelling pretty badly, and I had to keep them elevated. When I sat in the living room, I propped them on a pillow. I was unable to go outside on the sunny porch in the spring and summer, which was upsetting because those were my favorite seasons. I enjoy the sunshine beaming on me in the spring, but I couldn't sit in the sun because it irritated my skin.

I no longer attended church because it was too painful to sit on the pews. I watched Christian television shows to get a word from the Lord. I loved attending church and rarely missed unless I was very sick.

Some of the church members asked about me and wanted to visit. A few told my mother that they could convince me to go to the doctor. Mom warned them that my mind was made up and it would be hard to convince me. Nevertheless, they came, and I was ready. Whenever we expected visitors, Mom let me know so I'd have time to pray.

Yes, I prayed to God to help me tell them why I was walking by faith and trusting Him. I wasn't afraid to explain what God could do. I knew what I was up against, yet I wanted to be prepared, and God's Word was my weapon to fight off the doubters. I received weekly visits from members of the church, neighbors, and friends.

When Mrs. Inell Young, a neighbor and a member of the church, came to see me, she said that Luke was a physician.

"You are right," I said, "but Jesus is a healer."

I had to convince her I didn't have anything against doctors because I did go to doctors. It's not my job to discourage people not to go to doctors, but it is my job to recommend Jesus. I informed Ms. Inell that this was my choice, my spiritual encounter, and the vow I had made to God. I wanted to see if God could do this for me as He had for the ten lepers and Job.

While I talked to Ms. Inell, God put the words in my mouth, and she listened intensely. She had failed to convince me, but she was blessed by the words God gave me. I appreciated her concern and love.

Two weeks later, Ms. Marie Fornis and Ms. Susie Stewart, my other two godmothers, visited me. During my teenage years, these ladies were my best friends because I could share with them anything and everything, and not only were trustworthy, but they gave me so much wisdom. They came often to see me—not to convince me to change my mind and seek medical aid—but to hear the words God gave me about walking by faith. I had my first Bible study on my bed of affliction with these two ladies. As I shared the Word of God with them, they ate the bread of Life that sat before them. They were amazed at the knowledge God had given me. They listened and admired how I trusted God.

Day by day and week by week, people came, only to hear a young lady determined to walk by faith and not by sight. She trusted in God and didn't care whether they believed or not.

One particular visitor stood out the most, and that was Mr. Jack. Mr. Jack was a regular. He knew I loved fruit, and he brought me fruit baskets every other week. He tried to convince me to seek medical treatment, only to be rejected. He was a hard knot, and I was a hard believer.

Every time he visited, I put on my spiritual boxing gloves. Mom and Dad tried to warn him, but he kept trying and failing.

One day, I had a strange visit from Mr. Jack. Instead of a fruit basket, this particular time he entered the room with a large brown bag. I immediately saw a red flag but didn't make an issue. He explained the grocery store didn't have any fruit baskets, so he had picked out some fruit. When he handed me the large bag, he had a strange look upon his face. I was going to open the bag later, but he insisted I look inside.

I pulled out the fruit one by one and noticed a pink bottle at the bottom of the bag. When I withdrew the bottle, Mr. Jack's eyes shifted to the floor.

I screamed, "Mr. Jack Hughes! What is this!"

I couldn't believe how nervous he was when he explained the bottle was calamine lotion and that he wanted me to use it on my skin. He meant well, but I gave it back to him and said, "I'm trusting God, and He will do it." I had to convince Mr. Jack that God was a Healer and not a doctor. Doctors go to college and med school, God never did. God didn't need any help removing a rib from Adam's body to make Eve. The miracle worker removed it without any assistance.

Later, we laughed about the fruit basket incident. Mr. Jack continued to visit with fruit baskets and other sweet treats to get back on my good side. I was amused as there was no need for that, but he wanted me well and that was his way to help.

Within my heart, I felt that God didn't need any help. When God created the world in seven days, took the rib out of Adam and made a woman, and drove back the sea with a strong east wind, He didn't have any help **(Genesis 1-2/Exodus 14:21.)**

I figured God was doing all these miracles without the help of man, so He could do it for me, too. I also remembered what I had told God that night in the bathroom. God wants us to believe and have faith, and that was what I tried to do every day.

My purpose was not to convince people to never go to the doctors or to do what I was doing. My goal was to encourage others to try trusting and to have faith in Jesus when the doctors tell you there is nothing else they can do for you. What if you cannot get to the doctor or obtain medical services? I want people to know they can trust God.

Visitors kept coming and God kept talking, but no one could convince me to walk away from my journey. It was just Jesus and me.

If you can't pray it out, write it out. I was blessed with a journal in 1974 from a church member and immediately started my life of journaling. I documented my feelings and emotions, which helped me to release tensions the devil was fighting against my body. At times, journaling was my refuge.

When I tried to pray on rough days, sometimes I didn't know what to say. Have you been like that? I'd always said, "One day, I will write about this journey," but I'd never set a date or time. I used my journaling to talk to God on paper. I wrote him letters, telling him my true feelings, and it seemed as if everything was all right. Maybe the birth of a writer was beginning to come out of me.

Do you journal? It was a blessing for me.

CHAPTER THIRTEEN

Thumbelina

God will bring things to your remembrance. **"But the Comforter, which is the Holy Ghost, whom the Father will send in my name, he shall teach you all things, and bring all things to your remembrance, whosoever I have said unto you"** (John 14:26).

Many times, I've heard ministers tell us to have childlike faith. During my healing process, God taught me steps on how to wait patiently for my healing, how to focus, and other ways to receive my healing.

God reminded me of an incident that happened when I was around four years old. I had forgotten all about it, but God knows how to minister to us in time of need. In this particular incident, God taught me how to wait on Him with joy and great expectation.

Around 1960 and 1961, there was a popular doll, Thumbelina. I first learned about Thumbelina from the Danish author Hans Christian Andersen, who wrote a fairy tale about Thumbelina and her adventures with toads, moles, and beetles. I loved that book. I also watched the actor Danny Kaye play the life of Hans Christian Andersen in the movie where he sang a song about Thumbelina. So, trust me when I tell you that I was truly a Thumbelina fan.

At age four, Mom and Dad asked me what I wanted for Christmas. I said I wanted a Thumbelina doll. I had seen the commercials on television, and she looked like a real baby, with pretty eyes and rosy cheeks. When you wound the key in her back, she moved her head and wiggled her body like a newborn. If you pressed her chest, she sounded like a baby trying to speak. I desperately wanted Thumbelina, and my parents promised it for me for Christmas.

My parents always tried to live up to their promises. I had no reason not to trust them and believe them.

Faith is hoping with great expectation. When you know that you are definitely going to receive something, you tell others, especially if it's good news. Anyone with good news wants to tell everyone about it. What did the woman at the well do when she received good news from Jesus? She spread it!

I was that woman at the well. I told anyone who came my way about Thumbelina. I told neighbors, friends, family, the milkman, the mailman, church members, teachers at school, and Sunday school teachers. I was happy and joyful sharing my news.

See, when a person knows God is going to do what He promised, they are not ashamed to tell others, and they know He will come through. Abraham gave God the glory for what He was about to do, and so did I, though I didn't know it.

I saw strangers in stores and told them about Thumbelina when they spoke to me. I wasn't ashamed or scared if they thought I was crazy or believed me or not, as long as I believed it. If you are scared to tell someone that God is going to heal you when there are no signs or proof of healing, then you don't believe He will.

From January through September, I faithfully spread the news. I know my family was tired of hearing me talking about Thumbelina, but I was so excited. That's how we should be when we are waiting on God. Sickened of my joyful news day in and day out, my brothers had gotten weary. They ran from me when they saw me coming. I guess anyone would become tired hearing the name Thumbelina for almost nine months straight, but I couldn't let her rest.

I never doubted my parents the first time they promised me the doll. I believed them, and no one could shake me. That's exactly the way we should believe and trust God.

One morning in November of that year, Mom passed by my room while I was making the bed. She stopped and watched. If the bed was not made up properly, she would strip off the coverings and tell me to do it correctly. Her motto was, "If you do it right the first time, you won't have to do it again." Can you relate to that?

While she watched, she observed me doing something I normally wouldn't do and questioned me. "Delphine, why do you have that little pillow on the left side of the bed?"

I smiled and said the little pink pillow was Thumbelina's bed.

Mom shook her head.

What was I doing? I was making preparations to receive that which was promised to me. If you asked God for a child, "O barren woman, why aren't you decorating the nursery?" If you asked God for a husband or a wife, "Why aren't you picking out your wedding dress or calling a travel agent for your honeymoon?"

This is what faith does. Faith moves. It doesn't sit still. Why haven't you gone to that car lot or talked to that building contractor to pick out the car you told God you wanted or discussed the blueprint of your dream home?

Throughout the first three weeks of December, our home was screaming the name of Thumbelina. I counted down the days and was insanely wild as Christmas neared. I couldn't sleep and eat the three days approaching December twenty-fifth. I remember lying in bed the last day before Thumbelina was coming. I fluffed her pillow bed talked to myself about this little doll that would arrive the following day.

My family members peeked in and shook their heads before moving on. But I wouldn't let their faces discourage me.

You cannot let people discourage you. Keep believing and never let their words change your mind.

On Christmas Eve, Mom encouraged my brothers and me to go to bed early. I didn't need any encouraging; I wanted the next day to hurry and arrive, so I was first to go to bed.

Early Christmas morning, I woke smelling coffee from the kitchen and drooling to see Thumbelina. I leaped out of bed, raced down the hallway, and took a sharp left turn toward the big red box under the tree. After tearing the wrapping paper to pieces, I saw Thumbelina's face. I pulled her out of the box, wrapped her in my arms, and gave her a big kiss. I had my baby doll!

I thanked Mom and Dad for giving me the desire of my heart, and the rest of the day, it was just Thumbelina and me.

The Word of God tells us, **"Delight thyself also in the Lord; and he shall give thee the desires of thing heart" (Psalm 36:4).**

If I can believe my mother and father, why can I not believe God? There have been times after that incident when my parents couldn't give me my heart's desires. God is greater than my parents, and He allowed me to trust back then, so I can trust Him now.

CHAPTER FOURTEEN

I'll Kneel for You, Delphine

How I missed kneeling to pray. God hears our prayers whether we stand or kneel, but I hadn't been able to kneel because it was so painful. With my swollen legs and my body covered in sores, I couldn't wear print clothes or nylon stockings. The dye in clothing irritated my skin, and when I removed the nylon stockings, my skin stuck to the stockings and pulled off my legs. Mom went to a five and dime store to purchase cotton stockings, which helped somewhat.

I constantly read the Bible and shared my thoughts with others in Sunday school class, but unfortunately, I was unable to attend some Sundays because of the pain in my legs. I missed hearing others share their points of view.

I prayed for a prayer partner. I wanted someone to read the Bible with and share the Word of God because I was unable to attend Bible study and church service.

The counterfeit comes before the real. I learned that when you pray to God, the devil hears what you say, too. It's the devil's job to deceive us and cause us to miss out on what God has for us. Reading how the devil deceived Eve allowed me to do what the Word tells us in **Matthew 26:41: "Watch and pray, that ye enter not into the temptation."**

Several weeks after that prayer, the doorbell rang. I was home alone and struggled to walk to the door. Two men smiled and asked if I would mind them entering the house to share the Word of God.

Oh my God, I thought. *God has sent me someone to study the Bible with.* I was so excited and couldn't wait to get started.

The men talked about the Lord, and I was blessed by their words. When I shared my walk of faith, they abruptly stopped me. I was floored when they commented on my faith in God. They said God only healed in the Bible days and not in our time.

With swollen legs and my body still covered in sores, I boldly told them that wasn't true. I sat up in my chair and said, **"But he was wounded for our transgressions, he was bruised for our iniquities: the chastisement of our peace was upon him; and with his stripes we are healed"** (Isaiah 53:5).

I also added that the Bible says that Jesus was the same yesterday, today, and forever. He healed then, and He still heals now. There was no convincing me that God only healed in the Bible days. I knew these men were not sent by God.

After they left—I had politely escorted them to the door—I started chanting, "I **AM HEALED! I AM HEALED!**" It was no longer, "God is going to heal me," but "God is healing me."

I was blessed to attend church the following Sunday, and while I sat in Sunday school class, a six-foot-something attractive young man entered our class. *I know him!*

The man was Ray Dunn. I hadn't seen him in quite some time. He was the same age as my brother Anderson. I remembered my mother telling me that she and his mother had been expecting at the same time and shared the same room in the hospital. Anderson was born on September fifth, and Ray was born on the seventh.

Ray flashed a big smile and appeared happy to be in the class. He took over the class and blessed us in the Word. I was impressed by his love for God's Word and how he didn't mind talking about the Lord.

We collaborated on the Word briefly after class was dismissed, and I had never seen anyone more excited about God. Ray had just moved back from Michigan and was returning to his home church. He could sing, and that's how we connected. We were both lead singers in the church choir.

One evening after choir rehearsal, Ray stopped by the house to visit. My family enjoyed his presence. The evening ended with Ray and me talking about the Lord. I shared my testimony that I was waiting on the complete healing of God. He thought that was awesome and admired my faith and my patience. He wanted to be a part of my journey. He loved reading God's Word and talking about the Lord. We chose each other to be our prayer partners and to have a weekly Bible study together.

After every weekly choir rehearsal, Ray faithfully came to see me for Bible study. It was rewarding for him to bring me the Word because my body was in so much pain that I was unable to attend church. Ray taught and preached the Word to me on the weekdays.

One day, he suggested taking our Bible study to the park. I told him the sun irritated my skin and I couldn't go, that I was confined to the house and rarely went anywhere except church.

Fear had me in bondage, and Ray knew it. He said he would pray about it. He didn't want me going to church and not anywhere else.

He prayed for weeks and weeks, and one day, he asked if he could take me riding. I immediately said no. I was afraid. I didn't know Satan had put fear in my heart. Ray wasn't having it, and for the first time, I had a friend willing to fight the devil for me.

He convinced me to go, which wasn't easy because fear had a firm grip on me. He picked me up at the house and waited patiently for me to muster up the courage to go outdoors. I was horrified to go riding for thirty minutes. It sounds crazy, but I was a victim to fear, and it didn't want to let go.

One day, I took a leap of faith and agreed to go to the lake with him. As we rode in the car, I watched the scenery as if it was the first time seeing it. My body wasn't aching, and I enjoyed the view. When we arrived, I was afraid to sit at a picnic table, but it was fine. I realized then that Satan had robbed me of good days and good times.

Satan doesn't love you or me. He just wants our souls.

Ray and I had wonderful Bible studies around nature. We prayed together, and tears ran down our eyes when we talked about the glory of God. Today, I enjoy going to the park and reading the bible around nature—I owe that to Ray.

My parents thought the world of Ray, and his mother adored me. God ordained our friendship and spiritual relationship. I shared with Ray how I was tormented at night by the devil and couldn't sleep.

Ray and I visited my godmother Ms. Omah Lee. One particular visit stood out. We were in the den, and while Ray was glorifying God to the highest, his voice faltered and he fainted. I was shocked and looked at my godmother. She was calm and informed me that Ray had been slain in the Spirit.

I had never witnessed anyone slain in the Spirit. When Ray had lived in Michigan, he said he had received the Holy Ghost. I didn't understand much about receiving the Holy Ghost. It was all new to me.

As we prepared to leave, I wondered if Ray was capable of driving me home. I didn't know when this Holy Ghost would hit again, and I wanted to make it home safely. While I was getting in the car, I saw Ray having final words with my godmother.

I prayed mightily under my breath that Ray wouldn't pass out while driving. During the drive home, I didn't talk, but I silently prayed. Thank God, He heard me.

As Ray walked me to the door, he told me to sleep well. *Yeah right*, I thought, but I told him I would try.

The following morning, Mom woke me to say that Ray was on the telephone. He asked if I'd slept the previous night. I had to think about whether I had or not. He was glad when I told him I didn't remember waking.

After we hung up, the phone rang again. It was Omah Lee asking the same question Ray had just asked me. I told her I had slept well, and she immediately laughed and praised God.

Weekly, she and Ray telephoned and asked about my night. My answer was always "Yes, I slept through the night."

I was becoming curious. What was going on with the night reports?

My godmother called the next morning, and I stopped her before she could finish her question. "Ms. Omah Lee, what is with all these questions from you and Ray?"

She laughed and confessed that she and Ray had been praying that God would take their sleep so I could sleep.

I didn't know what to say. I finally said, "You two did that for me?"

She said they had gladly done it.

After our conversation, I called Ray and asked why they had done that.

He said, "That's what love does and that's what prayer partners do for one another. "

Back in the day, if you had a partner to pray with, we called them prayer partners. But my prayer partners were really prayer warriors.

One night, Ray came over, and we made plans to pray for each other. We did that from time to time. He always had me on the throne, praying constantly for me, and that particular night when he grabbed my hand to pray, I told him how I missed kneeling to pray. The rash covered my knees so badly that I could hardly bend them.

He knelt and said, "Don't feel bad. I'll kneel for you, Delphine."

I was so moved that I wept uncontrollably.

Ray, with his long hair, reminded me of Nick Ashford of the musical duo, Ashford and Simpson. As I watched him pray, the sweat fell down his face, and his hair lost their locks. He boldly called on the Master for his prayer partner, and I thanked God for sending me such a powerful prayer partner.

If you have a prayer partner, count yourself blessed.

CHAPTER FIFTEEN

I Blame You, Daddy!

Be careful what you tell your children. Daddy was a good father, and I highly respected him. He raised us the best he knew, and he did a good job. He made sure his children knew about Jesus, and that's what I loved about him.

I can truly say that God blessed me with good parents and a grandmother who believed in prayer. Prayer played an essential role in my home, as well as my grandmother's home.

Before my father married my mother, he was a sinner. I'm not familiar with that part of his life and heard about it through Mom and Dad and some of his buddies.

I only know the saved father, but one story mom related stuck with me. He had lied to my mother and told her he had religion. Back in the day, people asked, "Do you have religion?" instead of "Are you saved?" Mom married him because she thought he was saved.

I had heard my elders saying that a sanctified wife sanctified her husband. **"For the unbelieving husband is sanctified by the wife, and the unbelieving wife is sanctified by the husband: else were your children unclean; but now are they holy"** (I Corinthians 7:14).

Mom shared this story as a witness that, indeed, a sanctified wife does sanctify her husband. Times were hard. Daddy and some of the men in our community were laid off from their jobs. My two brothers were toddlers, and Daddy suggested that he and Mom should become bootleggers until he was called back to work. My father believed in taking care of and providing for his children.

His suggestion didn't sit well with my mother. She abruptly opposed the suggestion and told my father that God can and will make a way. Realizing she had married a sinner, Mom prayed to God to save my father. She never tried to force him to attend church; she only prayed.

My father never suggested my mother shouldn't go to church, but he wasn't a hypocrite. He knew he was a sinner and did not play with God. He told me he would not dare sit in the house of the Lord with beer on his lips, his clothes smelling like wine and cigarettes, and after spending most of the night drinking with the guys. He refused to go to church, pretending to be a Christian. I admired that and thanked God for that example.

Mom had another suggestion, which was truly due to the guidance and the leadership of the Lord. Mom and the wives of the other laid-off men baked goods, such as mini sweet potato pies, pecan pies, cakes, cookies, and teacakes. Nearby was a paper mill company that was still in operation, and these women knew what time the employees went for their lunch break. Mom and the rest of the women set up tables and sold their baked goods. That's what kept the bills paid until their husbands returned to work.

Thank God for the sanctified wife for setting a good example and led by God as to what to do. Mom didn't stop praying for God to save my father. I'm proud to say because of her constant prayers to God, years later my father confessed the Lord as his Savior. Ain't He good? God is good!

In the beginning, my father wasn't totally on board with me as it related to my healing process. He stood back and watched. In the end, he came on board. The first two years, our prayers clashed. He prayed to God to change my mind, and I was praying and confessing by His stripes that I was healed.

My healing process wasn't easy. I lost strength many times, but God was always there to assist me with His supernatural strength. It sort of reminded me when the devil tempted Jesus in the wilderness and he was weak, but the angels ministered unto him. **"And he was there in the wilderness forty days, tempted of Satan; and with the wild beast; and the angels ministered unto him" (Mark 1:13).**

I will never forget one particular night when I was brutally attacked by Satan with unbearable aches and pain. It was as though Satan had it in for me. Daddy was passing by my room and witnessed the torture. He was helpless. All I had was the Word of God to help me. I spoke Scriptures after Scriptures while the pain increased. Mom was in the room, witnessing the unpleasant moments. My parents watched their daughter calling on Jesus while suffering excruciating pain.

Daddy stood at the foot of the bed, looking at me with tears running down his eyes. My father did not cry easily. He dropped to his knees and prayed. Then, he stood and asked, "Why, Delphine? Why are you doing this to yourself?"

With pain shooting through my body, I managed to sit and yell, "I blame you, Daddy. You should never have told me how Jesus healed the sick and raised the dead because I believed you. I believe you then, and I still believe it!"

I wish I could describe the look on his face. He was stunned at my answer. He wasn't disappointed, but he looked at me for a few seconds in awe and went back on his knees. He didn't say anything while kneeling, but his lips moved.

I lay back in bed, and slowly, the pain left.

When Daddy stood, he looked at me with so much respect as though he was proud of me. It was a strange but memorable moment.

CHAPTER SIXTEEN

If I Die, I'll Die Believing God

DON'T LET SATAN GET INTO YOUR MIND! That is what I had to do.

Satan will tell you nothing but lies. If we spend the entire day listening to the devil's lies, we will never accomplish anything. It was in the early part of the third year, and my body wasn't improving. Everything was at a standstill.

The voice of Satan entered my mind, talking and speaking lies. How did I know it was Satan? Satan speaks what is contrary to the Word of God. The solution of not falling for his lies is to not believe anything he tells you. I read in the Bible, "**he was the father of lies, and he abode not in truth**" (John 8:44).

He lied to Eve in the garden, and she believed him. **Even him, whose coming is after the working of Satan with all power and signs and lying wonders. And with all deceivableness of unrighteousness in them that perish; because they received not the love of the truth,** that they might be saved. And for this cause God shall send them strong delusion, that they should believe a lie. That they all might be damned who believed not the truth, but had pleasure in unrighteousness (2Thessalonians 2:12).

Never entertain the devil. He will have you believe what he says and suggests is the truth. Judas and King Saul entertained the devil, and it cost them their lives. That's why so many people end up behind bars or do something horrible—because they listened to the voice of Satan. Once he has you believing him, he can captivate your mind so that you will believe his lies and your ears will no longer believe truth. That's why it is so important to know the Word of God and to know God. If you don't know God's Word, you don't know truth.

Why do so many people feel as if they are alone? Because they don't know that God's Word says that He will never leave them nor forsake them.

Get to know God. You need to know what He likes and dislikes. Learn about him, and when you do, you will know when and how the devil is deceiving you.

I was fully aware that I was in a spiritual warfare. I knew Satan hated me, but I did not know the depth of his hate. Satan had a deep hate for Jesus. He spoke to the minds of many to try to have Jesus killed before his birth. He knew Jesus' mission here on earth, and he didn't want it to come to pass.

The devil hates anyone who tries to live for Christ. His mission is to destroy us without mercy. **"Be sober, be vigilant; because your adversary the devil, as a roaring lion, walketh about, seeking whom he may devour" (I Peter 5:8).**

Satan loves to send all kinds of sickness and diseases to the body, and God loves to heal the body. Satan told me all kinds of lies, what God could not do and what He would not do for me. He spoke to me, saying that my feet and legs would always be swollen and that I would never wear high heels again.

I boldly said, "Oh yes, I will." I purchased high heels and kept them in the closet until I was able to wear them. Never allow Satan to dictate your destiny. God is in control of your life. Satan constantly told me I was going to die, but I boldly told him I shall live and not die!

Another incident occurred one night when my bones constantly ached and I had a bad headache. Satan spoke to me that I was going to die. He insulted me. O my, the devil loves to do that. "Look at you," he said. "Sores all over your body, and you say you're healed. You better get up from this bed and go to the doctor because you are about to die."

Do I have anything against doctors? No! I tried doctors before I tried Jesus, and I was willing to wait on the Healer I had made a promise to and see if He would perform what His Word said He could. The devil went on and on and on until I'd had enough. With pain shooting in my temples and other parts of my body, I managed to sit up in bed, ball my fist, and tell Satan he was a liar! I cried so loudly that my family members ran into the room because they thought I was screaming for them. I had to tell them I was talking to the devil.

Instantly, my mind went upon Meshach, Shadrach, and Abednego standing before the fiery furnace. Thank God for reading His Word, because His Word was where I pulled my strength. You have to know and read God's Word when you are fighting spiritual or natural battles because the flesh will let you completely down. I remembered those three fearless, bold, and courageous men who hadn't feared the king or the fiery furnace. They were steadfast, irremovable, knowing, and trusting their true and living God, and that's the pivotal solution in trusting God; you have to know whom you believe.

Apostle Paul said, **"For I know whom I have believed, and am persuaded that he is able to keep that which I have committed unto him against that day"** (II Timothy 1:12).

These valorous men were willing to lose their lives before they insulted their God and bowed to and worshiped a golden image. If we are in the flesh, we cannot please God, and these men were not in the flesh but in the Spirit. They were fighting a spiritual and natural warfare. These men boasted about their God to King Nebuchadnezzar by telling him that the God whom they served was able to deliver them from the burning fiery furnace and how He would deliver them out of his hand. That's what I call, "HOLY BOLDNESS" **(Daniel 3: 15-18)**.

I told that mean old devil, "I shall live and not die!" If God should take me home for trusting Him and believing Him, what a way to go, but I wasn't going to die. Dying was not in my thoughts at all. My faith was letting me know that God was healing me day by day. Although no proof or evidence existed, I was determined to stand and wait on God.

The Word of God told me in **Second Thessalonians 3:13: "Be not weary in well doing."** God was doing good work in my body and my spiritual body, and I couldn't give up. My spiritual body was my inner man, and as I walked in faith day by day, I was growing mightily in the spirit. I realized God was healing and delivering my spiritual body first, and my fleshly body would soon be healed.

My Bible tells me that **"death and life are in the power of the tongue and they that love it shall eat the fruit thereof"** (Proverbs 18:21). Stop allowing the enemy to conduct your life. Speak life over death. Speak life into your body, your mind, your heart and soul.

On one occasion, I had to speak healing over my brother Anderson. I noticed when he brought my lunch to my bed that his hands were breaking out as mine had. I was furious because I knew exactly what was going on. See, when you make a stand to serve God, Satan doesn't like it. He sees that he can't affect you, and then he attacks the one you love.

During my night prayer, I addressed Satan about what he was doing to my brother. I told Satan that this was my war, not his, and I asked God to heal my brother's hands. The following morning, I anointed his hands, and the next week God healed him.

Why not me? It wasn't my time. Was I disappointed? No. After months of walking in the Spirit, fasting for twenty-one days, praying and reading the Word of God, I knew God had to work on me a little while longer. In God's eyes, I wasn't ready. Whenever you seriously seek the Lord, He will show you things in the Spirit that a natural man or woman cannot see nor understand. Deep down in my heart, I knew God was changing me and I didn't mind waiting.

CHAPTER SEVENTEEN

I'm Using You. Come On, Jesus!

Deep down in my heart and soul, I knew God was healing me, but my flesh wanted to know how long it would take. My ears and neck were raw and breaking out, my face was twisting, sores were developing on my head, and my hair was falling out.

I talked to God one night as I sat in the middle of the bed. I wasn't afraid to ask God anything. It felt as though He was my friend and I could ask Him anything and at any time. I told him this journey we've been on is going on for three years. Yes, I said "we" because it was just us—just Jesus and me. I poured out my heart and soul to Him and let Him know that I knew he would heal me and not shame me amongst them that I had boldly witnessed to, but I needed to know whether I had missed something and if I needed to do anything.

As I sat in my bed, God revealed my sins that were not under His son's blood. I had to repent and forgive. You see, after reading God's Word daily and praying, I found my shortcomings. I was a church-going hypocrite. I wasn't living the life God wanted me to live. I was going to places and doing things that Jesus wouldn't do.

"Therefore if any man be in Christ, he is a new creature: old things are passed away; behold all things are become new" (2 Corinthians 5:17). Singing in the choir, paying tithes and offerings, and being a faithful member of a church yet living like the devil through the week doesn't mean a person is saved. Daddy's early years as a sinner taught me that. That's not the life of a Christian, either.

I tell people constantly that simply because you go to church it doesn't mean you are saved. You must be born again to enter into the kingdom of God. **"Jesus answered and said unto him, Verily, verily, I say unto thee, Except a man be born again, he cannot see the kingdom of God. Jesus answered, Verily, verily, I say unto thee, Except a man be born of water and of the Spirit, he cannot enter into the kingdom of God" (John 3:3, 5).**

I wasn't real with Christ. I was serving the devil and trying to serve God, too. **"You can't serve two masters. No man can serve two masters: for either he will hate the one, and love the other; or else he will hold to the one and despise the other" (Matthew 6:24).**

I could no longer continue in sin, and God was letting me know it. **"What shall we say then? Shall we continue in sin, that grace may abound? God forbid. How shall we, that are dead to sin, live any longer therein?"** (Romans 6:1-2).

I'm so grateful God revealed that to me because I thought I was saved, but I was not living a saved life. I was just going to church. Can you relate? I'm so glad the Word of God judged me, not man, but God Word judged me, found me, and saved me.

After deep soul-searching and crying out to God in true repentance, I asked God if there was anything else I must do. I wanted to get things right with God. **"Some men's sins are open beforehand, going before to judgment; and some men they follow after"** (I Timothy 5:24).

I wanted my sins and shortcomings revealed to me right then and there. I didn't want them revealed to me on Judgment Day, and I didn't want them following me. I could have gotten them under the blood. "God, tell me now while I have a chance to make it right with you. That person I hurt or mistreated and done wrong? Whatever Lord, Tell me!"

After spending days of repentance, I approached the Lord again, asking Him what else I must do and what else I needed to know. That night, God spoke to me plainly, saying, "I'm using you, to let people know, **I AM** a healer."

I repeated those words in my mind slowly, over and over again. I meditated on those words for a while. Later, I knew exactly what God was telling me. *Eureka!* I got it! If I'm to let people know that He is a healer, I have to be healed as living proof.

I praised God, and all of a sudden, it was like a bolt of faith entered into my heart. I cannot explain it. God gave me something special that night.

The other nights ahead were war. Satan launched so many blows at me that I couldn't understand them. Overnight sores popped up out of nowhere. Thank God I recognized what was going on. Satan was angry because his time of torturing and tormenting me was almost over.

My mother noticed new sores spreading when she aided me, and I laughed inside. When Mom left the room, I fought. I looked at the new sores the devil put on my body and asked, "Is this the best that you can do?"

The devil didn't like me talking like that. See, after God told me He was using me, I knew Satan was losing his battle and God was going to bring me out. Also, when the devil is revealed, he can't hide anymore, and he fights you.

Night after night, the devil attacked me with more sores. I laughed at him and told him to shoot his best shot. He was losing ground because I was loose from all the fears that had me bound. In the back of my mind, I knew God had my back, and I was not afraid of the terrors at night.

The devil kept fighting, but I kept fighting and continued to believe, and God helped me prevail over him. When you know your enemy and his weakness, you can defeat him. Satan knew my weakness was fear, and once God delivered me from fear, he was losing the battle.

God gave me joy in the fight. What is "joy in the fight"? I was defeating the devil and laughed at him constantly because God was backing me in the fight. Every day, it was as if I looked forward going into battle, and I went in with my battle axe, crowning the devil head with The Word of God. I thought about Samson when he killed a thousand men with the jawbone of a donkey. He was a one-man army.

Several months into the third year, the warfare was still going on. I was winning because the sores on my body were drying up. My body had turned to a dark coal-like color, but the pain wasn't hard to bear. I felt as if I was in a season of rest. I was sleeping better although I still had to fight Satan, but the battles were fading. I knew within my soul the journey was coming to an end.

It's hard to explain, but I had a peace and calmness in my soul. God's glory rested in my spirit, and my faith had elevated. I couldn't get that night God spoke to me out of my mind. That night transformed newness in my heart, mind, and soul. I didn't share that experience with anyone, not even my closest friends. I wanted to cherish that moment by myself for a while. That was an awesome night.

While listening to the radio one night, I heard a song by The Archers, "Make Me an Instrument." I wept like a baby because that song was my prayer to God. That night, I made that song my spiritual anthem. That was what I wanted to be for God—an instrument of His love.

One morning, I woke up facing my right wrist. My eyes were fixated on an area of my wrist that I didn't recognize. I pulled my wrist back from my face and examined a tiny area. Low and behold, I spotted a small patch of clear skin. I laughed and leaped for joy, screaming, "Come on, Jesus! Come on Lord!"

Slowly but surely, God was repairing my body. I beheld the healing power of Christ.

I didn't tell anyone. I didn't want to reveal myself to the world quite yet. I wanted others to notice the change. Week after week, I saw the skin of newness.

"Come on, Jesus! Come on, Lord! By his stripes, I am healed," I said daily.

I watched the sores diminishing, my hair restoring, my face twisting back into place, the boils making head and bursting on their own, and my skin turning back to its original shade. My family noticed the changes, too.

Yes, I was brand new! God not only healed me, but He also saved me. Salvation came to my home as it had come to the home of Zacchaeus. **"And Jesus said unto him, This day is salvation come to this house, forsomuch as he also is a son of Abraham. For the Son of man is come to seek and to save that which was lost" (Luke 19:9-10).**

Do I regret making that vow? Not at all. It was the best thing that had happened to me. I found a deliverer, and God placed my feet on the right road.

After my entire body had changed to newness, I asked God a question. "Who are you, Lord? You came and visited a woman on her bed of affliction and miraculously healed her."

I remember that night three years ago when I told God, "I don't know You as a healer. I only heard about You, but I don't know You like that." I asked God that night to prove Himself to me, and three years later, He did. Now I know the Lord is a healer.

Because God had done this for me, I asked Him, "What can I do for you?" I gave God my life. "I will let people know that You are a healer," I told Him. "Lord, to me, You are not a doctor, You didn't go to medical school, and You don't need me telling You what's wrong with me when I'm sick or hurting because You already know. After all, it was You who formed me in my mother's belly, and You created my organs and tissues." Lord, You are my Healer and my Creator.

CHAPTER EIGHTEEN

I Must Complete My Mission

After receiving the mighty miracle from God, I felt compelled to go out and share my testimony, which was like fire shut up in my bones. I needed to spread this fire with someone.

First, I shared it with my church family. I asked Reverend Martin, my pastor at that time, if I could speak before he gave his sermon. He agreed, and I couldn't wait. Although I was already a living testimony of God's healing as the church members had beheld my healed body, I wanted to share a small scale of my experience and thank those who had visited me.

When Reverend Martin made room for me to speak, I saw Mr. Jack weeping like a baby. Daddy and Mom sat proudly while I shared the awesome work of the Lord. Ms. Marie's and Ms. Omah's eyes filled with tears, and they wore joyful smiles as they beheld the glow that God positioned on my face.

After completing my testimony, Reverend Martin stood before the congregation and shared how he had advised me to go to the doctor but I had rejected his advice. I was startled by his confession. He said, as well, that I had made a believer out of him. Wow!

I beheld a man of God who was unashamed to tell his flock that he was wrong and lacked the faith and how, by my unmovable stand and trust in God, he became a believer of divine healing. I was moved by his honesty and had such respect for him. He didn't have to share it, but he thought it was necessary to do so. Poor Mr. Jack stood up, weeping uncontrollably, saying how he had sneaked the skin lotion into my room to try to help me and how he had to return home with it. We all had a good laugh about that.

It was time to hit the streets. I made a commitment to God to go out once a week and tell someone my testimony. We had three churches in my community: one Methodist church and two Baptist churches. I would find out who was on the sick and shut-in list who could not attend church, and I would visit them. The Bible tells us in James **5:14-16: "Is any sick among you? Let him call for the elders of the church; and let them pray over him, anointing him with oil in the name of the Lord. And the prayer of faith shall save the sick, and the Lord shall raise him up; and if he have committed sins, they** shall be forgiven him. Confess your faults one to another, and pray one for another, that ye may be healed."

I took my Bible and my olive oil and leisurely walked the streets, knocking on doors, reading scriptures, and praying for the sick. The joy Ray gave me when he entered my home was the same reaction when I entered their homes.

How the elderly and sick enjoyed that. They looked forward to my visits. Ray prayed and read the word of God to me, and I did the same for them. I did this faithfully until God led me to share my testimonies with women's ministries and other church events.

Even today, I still have Bible studies in homes and churches, and I share my testimonies on social media. This year, 2019, has been thirty-seven years since I've experienced the skin affliction, and it hasn't returned. "God, I am keeping my word to You, and I am letting people know, through my testimony, preaching, teaching, and in this book that You, indeed, are a Healer."

"Your testimonies are not just about you. They're about others who will walk in your shoes and need to know how to keep walking. Testimonies are to be shared, not to be stored."—Delphine Kirkland

About Delphine

Delphine Paige Kirkland was born and raised in Tuscaloosa, Alabama. She is a minister, Bible teacher, songwriter, Christian blogger, Christian vlogger, dessert baker, and has a Women's Jail Ministry in Linden, Alabama. Delphine loves to sing Christian and gospel music.

Delphine studied music at Birmingham Southern College, and her dream was to become a successful opera singer, but God had other plans. Although her dreams and goals were interrupted, she doesn't feel life treated her unfairly. She strongly believes it was the will of God and doesn't regret one moment that her dreams and goals were shattered, because she found a Savior in a way she would never have known.

Now, Delphine's goals in life are to keep writing books to encourage and help those who are struggling on their Christian journey. She is eager to share with the world her story of how she met a God of power and miracles.

Delphine is happily married. She and her husband, Ben, reside in Sweet Water, AL.

Connect with Delphine

You can follow Delphine on her Facebook page at From The Master's Table and on Instagram @fromthemasterstable and @I_prayandbake.

Made in the USA
Las Vegas, NV
26 March 2021

20219572R00066